MW01611931

Growing in the Prophetic

Growing in the Prophetic

Lloyd C. Phillips

Essence
PUBLISHING

Belleville, Ontario, Canada

Growing in the Prophetic

Copyright © 2002, Lloyd C. Phillips

All Scripture quotations, unless otherwise specified, are from the *New King James Version*. Copyright © 1979, 1980, 1982. Thomas Nelson Inc., Publishers.

ISBN: 1-55306-410-0

Previously Published under ISBN: 1-885-10185-6
Copyright © 2000, Lloyd C. Phillips

Essence Publishing is a Christian Book Publisher dedicated to furthering the work of Christ through the written word. For more information, contact: 44 Moira Street West, Belleville, Ontario, Canada K8P 1S3.
Phone: 1-800-238-6376. Fax: (613) 962-3055.
E-mail: info@essencegroup.com
Internet: www.essencegroup.com

Printed in Canada
by

Essence
PUBLISHING

"Worship God!
For the testimony of Jesus
is the spirit of prophecy."

Table of Contents

Introduction

BEING A GRACIOUS SAVIOR, the Lord has made available wisdom, knowledge, and understanding to His people so that they need not be in the dark concerning spiritual matters relating to their lives. The purpose, then, of the information presented here is to assist His people in better understanding the prophetic operation of the Holy Spirit, whether they have a prophetic "gifting" or not. I have attempted to write in such a manner that the information will mentor the gifting in those who have it, whether or not they are called to the level of the "office of a prophet." There are different applications biblically for using the term *prophet*. I believe that in our administration of grace all Christians potentially have the ability to prophesy regularly if they have pursued the gift and received it through humility. All Christians with the spirit of Christ are, in a special sense, "prophets, priests, and kings" (1 Cor. 14:31; Rev. 1:6) because we have the spirit of our Prophet, Priest and King, Jesus Christ. Therefore, in a simple sense, anyone who prophesies may be called a prophet at a certain level biblically. However, culturally, to make things more clear and avoid unnecessary confusion, we often refer to a person prophesying at the level of the simple gift of prophecy as a "prophetic person." There is a gift ministry of a prophet, often referred to as the office of a prophet (Eph. 4:11), which is quite different and has many additional and strict responsibilities from "one who prophesies."

In this writing, I have attempted to include information which will assist those called to function in either category. It's my purpose to share information which will benefit and help to mature the operation of the gift, always keeping in mind that there is a difference in levels of authority and application. Distinctions are made to help those who are called to the higher responsibility of the ministry of the prophet. However, most often when referring to a prophet in this writing, the term *prophet* can be used in the simplest form of "one who prophecies."

I would like to further explain to the reader a major distinction that I see between these two levels of the prophetic. Those who operate in the simple gift or evidence of prophecy BRING A GIFT to the Church through the spirit in them. Those called to the gift ministry of a prophet ARE A GIFT to the Church. The Lord has given their lives as gifts of service to the people of God. It is my hope that the information contained in this writing will be expounded upon by The Teacher—who is the Holy Spirit—as you read and will be of service to those who are called to edify and build up the Church at every level of the prophetic.

....

Chapter 1

Perceptions
of the Prophetic

SOME PEOPLE BELIEVE that many years ago God talked until His bestselling book was completed and then stopped speaking. This was not the case. If we believe the Scriptures were written as men were inspired by the Holy Spirit (2 Pet. 1:21), then we must also admit that the same Spirit is here today. God is eternal and does not change (Mal. 3:6). The same prophetic gift is available today—not for the writing of Scripture, mind you, but for communicating with His family. His Word is a lamp unto our feet and a light unto our path, and any true prophetic word is a word from God and should be treasured as such. The same vehicle of utterance is used in both cases.

The Word of God (i.e. the Bible) is our "more sure word of prophecy" (2 Pet. 1:19). All prophecy should be judged according to Scripture. Any prophetic utterance which appears to contradict the Word of God should be held suspect. Any word which clearly contradicts Scripture should be rejected immediately. Notwithstanding, sometimes we need a specific word from God to lead us in an obedient lifestyle following the teachings of Scripture. For example, Matthew 4:4 says that man shall not live by bread alone, but by every word that proceeds from the mouth of God. The Greek word translated as "word" here is *rhema,* which is an utterance or spoken word, as opposed to *logos,* translated word when the written Scripture is referred to. Where would the apostle Paul be if the Lord had not spoken directly to Ananias and said, *"Go out your door, turn on the street called Straight, and minister to a man named Saul"* (Acts 9:11)? Where would Ananias go to find these instructions in Scripture? God is the same God today as He was then. He will speak just as specifically to us today as He did then. We can expect to see the same manifestations of prophecy today as the early church saw two thousand years ago.

A true prophetic word can prepare us for the future. The reason we find ourselves unprepared in a given situation is because we often are not hearing from the Lord, and therefore, we are not walking prophetically. We are not listening to the prophetic word nor receiving the prophetic word. Romans 10:17 says that faith comes by hearing the *rhema* word of God. Scripture says the Holy Spirit will show us things to come (John 16:13). We are all prophets in the sense that we all may prophesy because we all have the Spirit of God. We do not have to be prophets in the five-fold apostle, prophet, evangelist, shepherd, teacher sense, but we all have the spirit to prophecy. So, we may speak the oracles of God (1 Pet. 4:11). Every Christian has this potential.

Chapter 2

What Can the Prophetic Word Do for Us

FIRST, THE PROPHETIC WORD gives us wisdom. Specifically, the number one type of wisdom a prophetic word brings is vision. When there is no vision, we become easily distracted, and distraction leads to discouragement. Discouragement leads us to deception, and deception leads us to destruction. Without vision, we fall into this destructive cycle, but when we receive vision from the Lord, we break the cycle. Proverbs 29:18 says, *"Where there is no revelation (or vision) the people cast off restraint. But happy is he who keeps the law."* The people are perishing for lack of vision. Some have suggested that the prophetic is unnecessary as long as we are manifesting the love of God. First Corinthians 12:31 says, *"But earnestly desire the best gifts. And yet I show you a more excellent way."* The better way is love, but Paul is not saying here that if you have love you should not have the gifts in operation. We need the gifts in operation. He says to "earnestly desire," to covet after the best gifts, which are those gifts that can bring blessings. If you really walk in love, you will desire those gifts to bless others. Love has an attitude of service towards others, and the apostle Paul said, *"Even so you, since you are zealous for spiritual gifts, let it be for the edification of the church that you seek to excel"* (1 Cor. 14:12). We are to be zealous for spiritual gifts, but not as those in the Corinthian church who were desiring them for their own selfish promotion. Instead, Paul wanted them to desire the gifts for the purpose of edifying the Church. Paul said, *"Pursue love and desire spiritual gifts, but especially that you may prophesy"* (1 Cor. 14:1). The context here is in the church service setting. In the church setting, we especially ought to have prophecy because it builds up the Church. It brings the word from heaven to our ears.

First Corinthians 14:39 says, *"Therefore brethren, desire earnestly to prophesy and do not forbid to speak in tongues"*— especially if we interpret because we are edified as we receive the word from heaven. Forbid not to speak with tongues. Desire earnestly to prophesy. Some people do not like the instructions contained in this verse. There are entire denominations that effectively cut it out of the Scriptures. I do not think it should be cut out. It was put in there by God for a reason, and it is just as valid today as the day it was written. We should desire earnestly to prophesy. The gifts are given by the choice of God and according to His will (1 Cor. 12:11, 28). These gifts are activated by our faith. If they

18

are not in operation, it is due to our faith. Information may help our faith (faith comes by hearing). James 4:6 says, *"But He gives more grace. Therefore He says: 'God resists the proud, But gives grace to the humble.'"* The gifts in 1 Corinthians 12 are the grace gifts or empowerments. The word *gifts* comes from the Greek word *charis*. The word *charisma*, from which we get our word *charismatic*, stems from the word *charis*, which corresponds to our word *grace*. The way we receive those gifts humbles ourselves before the Lord because He gives grace to the humble. If we will use what He has given us, He will be faithful to give us more. So, we can all have these gifts in operation at one time or another. Scripture says that He gives these graces according to His will. Our task, then, is to put ourselves in a position of humility and service towards others so that it becomes His will to give these graces to us. He always desires to give good gifts to His children (Matt. 7:11, Luke 12:32).

The second effect a prophetic word can have is to bring testimony and confirmation from God to man. First Corinthians 14:3-5 states:

> *But he who prophesies speaks edification and exhorta-tion and comfort to men. He who speaks in a tongue edi-fies himself, but he who prophesies edifies the church. I wish you all spoke with tongues.*

God says He wants us all to speak with tongues, but even more He desires that we prophesy. Does this mean we should do one but forget the other? Absolutely not. What, then, should we be doing in our private lives? Pray-ing in tongues like a house on fire! Speaking in tongues much! As we speak in tongues frequently, we will receive a word from time to time to bring to the Church through prophecy or interpretation. *"For he who prophesies is greater than he who speaks with tongues, unless indeed he interprets"* (1 Cor. 14:58). This is saying that prophecy and interpretation of tongues are equal to one another in ability to serve the congregation. So, when someone speaks in tongues and brings the interpretation, that word is, to our ears, the same as prophecy because it is a word from the Lord that we can understand, discern, and put into practice. It is a word from the Lord, from God to man, given so that the Church present may receive edification.

There is a difference between the office of a prophet and those who prophesy. Simply because one prophesies does not mean that he has the burden, mantle, authority, or call of a prophet. If those kinds of words are received by a true prophet in a place or congregation where there is no established relationship with the leadership, rather than give a proclamation, it would be proper to speak to the leadership privately or simply pray.

First Corinthians 1:4-7 states:

I thank my God always concerning you for the grace of God which was given to you by Christ Jesus, that you were enriched in everything by Him in all utterance and all knowledge, even as the testimony of Christ was confirmed in you, so that you come short in no gift, eagerly waiting for the revelation of our Lord Jesus Christ.

There are a number of interesting things in this section. One, prophecy brings the testimony of Christ. It will confirm things the Holy Spirit has been speaking previously. Two, it will help us to not come short in any gift. The reason many of us are not walking in all the gifts is because we have neglected prophecy. The reason we do not know the testimony of Jesus is because we have neglected prophecy. The reason we are in such need of confirmation in our lives is because we have neglected the prophetic word. The reason the 900 numbers for "psychic" hot lines and tarot card readers are making so much money in our world today is because people want to hear a good word, even if it is a false good word. They want some confirmation in their lives, even if it involves going in the wrong direction. If the Church will again begin to practically function in the gifts that God has given us, then the world will have the true light available to confirm and direct. Revelation 19:10b declares, "... *for the testimony of Jesus is the spirit of prophecy.*" I want to hear what the Lord is saying. What is His testimony in His Church? What is He doing? What is the Spirit saying to the Church today? How can we have Him as our Head if we will not listen to what He is saying? The testimony of Jesus is the spirit of prophecy. The testimony of Jesus confirms and enriches. Prophecy will bring us into grace and grace brings us His gifts.

It has been said that if a prophetic word does not confirm, it is not true. This is incorrect. Many times, a word will come and it will be the first time it is heard. Confirmation can come at some later time. Please do not think that every word has to be confirmed to be from God. Every true word will be confirmed if we remain faithful, but let's try not to put God in a box. Often, the confirmation comes when the results of obedience are apparent, and that may be the only confirmation God allows. The prophetic word is not always confirmation, but God will always reward obedience to His word. An example of this is found in Acts 11:27-30, where the prophet Agabus prophesied a famine. The people were obedient to plan accordingly and were blessed because they obeyed in faith. The confirmation occurred when the famine arrived, but they were blessed through obedience. God also says that out of the mouth of two or three witnesses every *rhema* word is established (2 Cor. 13:1).

Genesis 41:32 is the first example of the confirmation of a twice spoken word. Joseph was speaking to Pharaoh.

And the dream was repeated to Pharaoh twice because the thing is established (confirmed) by God, and God will shortly bring it to pass.

By the Rule of First Mention, the principle that the first mention of something sets a pattern for subsequent uses throughout the rest of Scripture, we know that this verse gives definition to the meaning of something "twice given" and sets it throughout the Word of God. If a word is given once and is confirmed by a second mention, it will absolutely happen. Another example is found in Acts 15:32: *"Now Judas and Silas, themselves being prophets also, exhorted and strengthened."* "Strengthened" is the Greek word *episterizo*, which in English is "to be confirmed." In the King James version of the Bible, it says, *"they confirmed… the brethren with many words."* What kind of words were they speaking? They were prophets. They were speaking prophetic words to confirm the saints.

Prophecy is also used in spiritual warfare. In talking to his spiritual son Timothy, Paul said,

This charge I commit to you, son Timothy, according to the prophecies previously made concerning you, that by

them you may wage the good warfare... (1 Tim. 1:18).

The prophecies spoken over Timothy gave him vision and direction, and he was able to fight a good spiritual warfare. Ephesians 6:12 says,

For we do not wrestle against flesh and blood, but against principalities, against powers, against the rulers of the darkness of this age, against spiritual hosts of wickedness in the heavenly places.

"We are mighty through God to the pulling down of strongholds with the weapons of our warfare" (2 Cor. 10:4). Prophecy is a weapon of warfare.

The third aspect a prophetic word can fulfill for us is prosperity. Ezra 6:14,

So the elders of the Jews built, and they prospered through the prophesying of Haggai the prophet and Zechariah the son of Iddo. And they built and finished it, according to the commandment of the God of Israel, and according to the command of Gyrus, Darius, and Artaxerxes king of Persia.

They prospered because of prophecy. It was not just the prophetic words that caused them to profit; it was the prophetic word acted upon that prospered them. They believed those words, and they acted on them. Faith without works is dead. If we hear a word and have faith in that word, we need to act. As I referred to earlier, Agabus prophesied to the saints in Antioch that there was going to be a famine which would effect all of the world. Their response was, "Oh, we'd better take up a collection to help out in Judah's famine." Consider, though, that famines do not happen over night. Even if the rain had stopped the next day, it would not have been a famine yet. It would become a famine when the crops failed and the food ran out. Yet, Agabus prophesied, and they immediately took up a collection. Every man gave as he could. Their response was significant. Most people upon hearing of a possible famine would begin to stock up or even hoard, but their response was to give according to their ability. By the prophetic word which came to them, God was able to prosper them through their giving and those in Judah through the gifts.

The fourth function that the prophetic word fulfills is to help us discern between good and evil. Hebrews 5:14 says,

> But solid food belongs to those who are of full age, that is, those who by reason of use have their senses exercised to discern both good and evil.

As we grow in the prophetic, it becomes clearer what is light and what is darkness. Malachi 3:14-15 says,

> You have said, "It is useless to serve God; What profit is it that we have kept His ordinance, and that we have walked as mourners before the LORD of hosts? So now we call the proud blessed, for those who do wickedness are raised up; They even tempt God and go free."

Many Christians today are of the same opinion. They see people prospering who are evil. They see those who curse God and apparently suffer no consequences. They see ministers of God who abuse the people and abuse the finances and yet appear to go unpunished. Those who do wickedness are raised up, and those who even tempt God go free. In Malachi 3:16 we read,

> *Then those that fear the Lord spoke to one another and the Lord listened and heard them. So a book of remembrance was written before Him for those who fear the Lord and who meditate on His name.*

Even when it appears that those who do evil are prospering, God is listening to you. Will we continue to proclaim what His word says? Will we continue to pray for the healing of our land, asking for mercy rather than wrath and judgment? If we will speak these things, He will write it in the book of remembrance because He is listening to us. Malachi 3:17-18 says,

> *"They shall be Mine," says the Lord of hosts, "On the day that I make them My jewels, and I will spare them as a man spares his own son who serves him. Then you shall again discern between the righteous and the wicked, between one who serves God and one who does not serve Him."*

As we continue to speak the words, we will be able to see what is right and what is wrong. The prophetic word will help us discern and help us divide between truth and error.

Prophecy is not criticism. Nor is it accusation. I know of a man who has a prophetic call on his life and yet has such an accusative spirit, especially towards leadership. He told me about a woman who prophesied over him saying that he had a critical spirit. I knew the young man well enough to believe that this was true. He went on to say that he cynically asked her to cast it out of him if that were the case. Nothing happened because it was not something that could be cast out in this case. The spirit of criticism by which he was influenced was an unmentored prophetic call. Unfortunately, many times when the Lord shows us something or brings it to us, we become critical rather than lifting it up to the Lord in intercession. Our response should be to take it to the Lord to find out what can be done. But, if we become critical, we cut ourselves off from walking further or deeper into that calling. Unless we will allow ourselves to come under submission and to have some coaching, it may be very difficult to break out of this. Often, a person in that position becomes bitter because he feels rejected. Often, he is rejected because he is critical. Who wants to hear a critical spirit come through a prophecy? We want to hear the testimony of Jesus. It must be understood that prophecy is not criticism; it is not accusation. Effectively, it should cast down the accuser of the brethren. True prophecy will always cut the purposes of the devil off, not bring him in and give him a place to preach. A prophetic utterance is strictly that—there is no authority attached to the application of the word. If this is not understood, the messenger may become embittered if he perceives that the word is not received by being acted upon. If it is not understood that the responsibility of the messenger ends with the delivery of the message, then there may be a temptation to influence or even manipulate the interpretation or application.

The fifth purpose we find is that the prophetic word is the voice of God on earth and it will bring us His counsel.

For the Lord has poured out on you the spirit of deep sleep, and has closed your eyes, namely, the prophets;

and He has covered your heads, namely, the seers (Isa. 29:10).

If we do not allow the prophetic in, our congregations will be in darkness. In the days of Eli, it says that "the lamp of God had gone out" because there was no prophetic voice. We need the seers. We need the prophetic word so that the eyes of the Church will be opened. Paul said, *"Can the eye say to the hand I have no need of you?"* (1 Cor. 12:21). Absolutely not. So, when we say we do not need the eyes of the Body of Christ, what are we saying? We are going against the Word of God, and here in Isaiah, the Lord took out their eyes because of the same disobedience.

The prophetic word is the voice of God. Prophecy will plant the supernatural. It germinates, it activates, and it releases His power. It is the declaration and the release of the seed of God's Word and His will. In 1 Kings, we see this with Elijah many times. In one example, the word of the Lord came to Elijah and said, "Pray that it will not rain." Elijah, then, said to King Ahab, "It is not going to rain at all except at my word." Just one day previously, Elijah could not have said that by his word God was not going to let it rain. It had to originate with God and come to Elijah by the word of the Lord. It could not have originated with Elijah. However, when that word came to him, it had to be spoken in order for it to come to pass. God gives authority to those who will speak prophetically. More authority will be given as we consistently speak His word from pure vessels. *"Surely the Lord GOD does nothing, unless He reveals His secret (plans) to His servants the prophets"* (Amos 3:7). God is sovereign. He has decided to do nothing without sharing His secrets and His plans with His servants who will speak forth prophetically from the secret places or from the house tops. Jesus said to His disciples, *"The things I am whispering in your ear you proclaim them from the housetops"* (Matt. 10:27). There were other times when Jesus said, "Do not tell a soul." We need to know when to give a word and when to forbear. If He gives a secret and it is not time to reveal it and we blab it, then we have just limited the authority which the Lord will delegate to us. This moves us into a lower level of trust. We need to remember He is our Father. He is also a mighty good general. He intends to win the spiritual battle. He gives us tests to see what we will do with His secret plans. Will we believe them and keep them to ourselves until told otherwise?

Rick Joyner says the true essence of prophetic ministry is to be so close to the Lord that He does not want to do anything without sharing it with you. More than anything else, the essence of prophetic ministry is to be a special friend and confidant to the Lord. Therefore, friendship and intimacy with Him must always be the primary and ultimate goal. Ultimately, He has called us as children, not as servants. We were called to be sons, but we learn through servanthood. As sons grow up and mature, they become friends (Gal. 4:1; John 15:15).

Luke 1:37 says, *"For with God nothing will be impossible."* The literal translation of this says, *"For with God no word spoken by Him is without power."* We are the voice of God on this earth. When we speak prophetically, it is the word of God and it has power. When Elijah received the word by standing in the presence of God and the Lord said, "Go pray and I will withhold the rain for three years," Elijah spoke it and it came to pass. Elijah stood in the counsel of

God with power, and God performed the word spoken. First Kings 17:1 says,

> And Elijah the Tishbite, of the inhabitants of Gilead, said to Ahab, "As the LORD God of Israel lives, before whom I stand, there shall not be dew nor rain these years, except at my word."

At first glance, this seems arrogant. Did it come to pass? Yes, and it was by Elijah's word. Even if he'd had some machine to turn off the rain, do you think he could have gone out there and turned off the dew? The phrase "before the God whom I stand" is spoken many times by Elijah. He had learned to stand in the presence of God and receive the counsel of the Lord such that, when he spoke the words of God, Elijah's word was law in the heavens. When he spoke it, the angels went out to do his word because he stood in the counsel of God. Do not become arrogant and think that just because you said it God has to bring it to pass. This is a dangerous presumption. When you stand in His counsel, He will do it because you are a co-worker with Him—you are His friend.

> So shall My word be that goes forth from My mouth; It shall not return to Me void, but it shall accomplish what I please, and it shall prosper in the thing for which I sent it (Isa. 55:11).

"Then the LORD said to me, 'You have seen well, for I am ready to perform My word'" (1 Jer. 1:12). The Lord asked Jeremiah, "What do you see?" Jeremiah told Him what he saw. God said, "Yes, that is right, and I am going to bring it to pass. I will perform My Word."

Sixth, prophecy is the expression of the heart and mind of God by a supernatural means. Terry Virgo said a truly prophetic person must be willing to live in the limitations of tent dwellings while looking for the city whose maker is God. Scripture says that Abraham was a prophet. It says that he was a friend of God. Yet, Abraham prophesied nothing which is recorded in Scripture. What did he do that made him a prophet? He was a friend of God. He stood in the counsel of the Lord, and he interceded. He prayed. He searched for a city whose maker was God, and he is in the Hebrews 11 "Faith Hall of Fame." He never received what was promised to him during his lifetime, but he remained faithful.

The Seventh dimension of prophecy is that prophecy and intercession are twins. Genesis 20:7 is another example of the Rule of First Mention. *"Now therefore, restore the man's wife; for he is a prophet."* This was God speaking to Abimelech concerning Abraham. God said, "Abraham is a prophet, and he will pray for you." This is the first verse in the Bible that has the word *prophet* in it, and it also happens to be the first verse in the Bible that has the word *pray*. This suggests a truth that holds throughout the Scriptures, namely that prophecy and intercessory prayer are twins and often overlap. We see in Scripture non-prophets that go into prophecy as they pray, and we see prophets who are great intercessors because the spirit of prophecy leads them into intercession.

> *For he is a prophet and he will pray for you and you shall live. But if you do not restore her, know that you shall surely die, you and all who are yours* (Gen. 20:7).

Jeremiah 27:18 states,

But if they are prophets, and if the word of the LORD is with them, let them now make intercession to the LORD of hosts....

Sometimes, a spirit of criticism tries to imitate or masquerade as a spirit of prophecy, but a true prophet takes a word back to the Lord and intercedes with it. If you desire to operate accurately in the prophetic, then bring it back to Him in intercession without boasting. True strength comes from relationship with the Lord, not from the motivation of what others might think.

The Eighth precept is that there is only one requisite in order to prophesy after we are saved in the name of the Lord Jesus. It is very simple: the ability to speak. All can prophesy. First Corinthians 14:31 states, *"For you can all prophesy one by one, that all may learn and all may be encouraged."* Anyone who is saved and has the Spirit of God has the latent ability to prophesy.

In regard to receiving prophecy, Jesus said anyone who receives a prophet because he is a prophet will receive a prophet's reward (Matt. 10:41a). To receive the rewards of prophecy, you must receive a prophet as a prophet. We are currently experiencing a restoration of the prophet ministry in the Body of Christ. The Church has wanted to receive words from the Lord and wanted to receive prophecy, but in order to receive the rewards, you have to receive the prophet in the name or authority of the prophet. This holds true for all ministries. The Church has taught a non-biblical standard for judging the apostolic and the prophetic, which has not been applied to the other ministries of shepherd, evangelist and teacher. The Church will not move into prophetic maturity if she is not willing to allow prophetic immaturity. In the Old Testament allowances were made for the sons of the prophets to grow, something the church in our day has not been willing to do. Prophecy cannot be judged until it is given. The Church today seems to want to judge the prophecy before it is spoken. Because of this, we do not receive the rewards of a prophet because we will not receive the prophet. We want the rewards, but we do not want to take the risks. In short, we want the cake and to eat it too. Sometimes, a prophecy might contradict a specifically held doctrine. The answer is not to immediately stone the prophet. Rather, go back to the Scriptures to verify the doctrine. In many cases, it has been found that the doctrine was incorrect. The prophecy cannot be judged before it is given. If the prophetic word truly does contradict sound doctrine, can't we allow the young prophet to grow and correct the word? We must, or else we will never reap the rewards of the prophet.

....

Chapter 3

Developing Prophetic Character

CHARACTER IS ACTUALLY integrity. Integrity means steadfast adherence to a state of being unimpaired, sound, the quality or condition of being whole, undivided or complete. As Christians, we are supposed to have a higher standard than the world. Prophecy is influenced by our soul nature and by our personality. We, therefore, must make every effort to submit ourselves to the character of Christ within us. This is a process called the salvation of the soul (1 Pet. 1:9). Allowing the Holy Spirit within us to transform our soul into the holiness of God allows our character to be Christlike. It is important to understand that the character we exhibit affects the words that we bring from the Lord. It is important to recognize the vessel that is speaking a prophetic word. Anything God gives through someone is coming through a human filter, and we do not want to filter out His intentions or His message. He chose to put these treasures in earthen vessels. He chose to pour the Holy Spirit into us so it would pour out from us. Out of our bellies will flow rivers of living water (John 7:38).

There is a difference between a prophet and a prophetic person. It is a difference in intensity and responsibility as well as a difference in calling. Someone who is called to walk in what we would identify as the office of a prophet is distinct from someone who has the gift or empowerment of prophecy in operation. We all may prophesy, as Paul said in 1 Corinthians 14:5. We all have the spirit of prophecy which is the Holy Spirit. Luke 2:21-40 contains an example of both gifts in operation. In this passage, Jesus was eight days old and Mary and Joseph had taken Him to the temple to be dedicated. Simultaneously, the Holy Spirit had led an old man named Simeon to speak prophetically over the Child. As he was speaking, a prophetess named Anna entered and heard the words that were being spoken by Simeon. She immediately began to herald them. Simeon was not a prophet. It says he was a "just and devout man," but he was not a prophet. In this situation, the prophetess was not called upon to bring forth the prophecy. But, when Anna heard the word, she discerned immediately that it was the word of the Lord. In verse 36, it says,

> Now there was one, Anna, a prophetess, the daughter of Phanuel, of the tribe of Asher. She was of a great age, and had lived with a husband seven years from her virginity.

If she was married when she was between thirteen and seventeen years old, which would have been customary, and then remained married for seven years, and then spent eighty-four years in the temple after her husband died, this would make her between 104 and 108 years old. So, of the 400 years between the Old and New Testament, it is reasonable to assume that for at least 104 of them, Anna was alive, and for the majority of them, she would have been operating as a prophetess. In my studies, every commentary I have ever read on the subject has said there was no prophet between the prophet Malachi and John the Baptist. However, the Bible is very clear that Anna was a prophetess during these years, and where the spirit of prophecy exists, the word of the Lord may be revealed. Anna arrived just as Simeon prophesied the blessing over Jesus and His mother.

And coming in that instant she gave thanks to the Lord, and spoke of Him to all those who looked for redemption in Jerusalem (Luke 2:38).

In this record, we see both the spirit of prophecy and the office of a prophetess working together with great humility. I can identify twelve major attributes of prophetic integrity, all of which Anna exhibits.

1. Humility

This is a bedrock necessity, a fruit of the Spirit for all Christian life but a must if we are going to walk prophetically. It is foundational. Humility is not low self-esteem. Low self-esteem originates in fear and pride. Humility is not only an absence of pride or doubt, but an absence of self. It is freedom from a preoccupation with self. Humility is a balance between pride and doubt. It is a place of knowing that without Him we can do nothing, but through Him we can do all things. Humility places us in a position to receive the grace to accomplish for God what we cannot accomplish for Him ourselves. Sometimes, true humility can be construed as terribly arrogant. Occasionally, God may ask us to say and do things that can make others think, "Well, who does he think he is? He's thinking of himself more highly than he ought." We must be truly humble and obedient in our hearts, knowing that it is not by our works or abilities that we are able to accomplish the Lord's directives. True humility is something that will set us apart from the world.

2. Hearing the Voice of God

Jesus said, "*My sheep hear My voice, and I know them, and they follow Me*" (John 10:27). It is possible for all born again believers to hear the voice of the Lord. In Jeremiah 23:22-23, it says,

> But if they had stood in My counsel, and had caused My people to hear My words, then they would have turned them from their evil way and from the evil of their doings. Am I a God near at hand, says the LORD, and not a God afar off?

In other words, God is saying, "Am I a God only for today and not also for tomorrow? Can I just give you a word for today but not also for down the road?" Of course He is eternal, the same yesterday, today, and tomorrow. He is saying, "Listen; I can tell you what is coming, and I can tell you how to prepare." We need to hear His voice in order to receive His counsel. Not every prophet will prophesy future events, i.e. foretelling. As was mentioned earlier, Abraham is an example of a prophet who did not prophesy anything about the future. He did hear things which were for the future, as when the Lord said to him, "*You shall be a father of many nations*" (Gen. 17:4). He did have a prophetic vision in his heart concerning the promise given to him (Heb. 11:13). But, nowhere is it recorded that he prophesied concerning those things. We should not put people, or their offices, in a box. If we are called, we are called to obey and do what God has called us to do. Simeon heard the voice of God, and he came. Anna heard the voice of God, and she came. Anna was not the one to prophesy at that time, but Simeon, who was not called as a prophet, did. Both were obedient to hear and obey the will of the Lord, and the prophetic word was acquired, accepted, and announced.

3. Obeying the Voice of God

To hear is one thing; to obey is another. When the Lord spoke to Ananias instructing him to go and minister to Saul, Ananias said, "Absolutely not! I am not going to go talk to him. Don't You know about him, Lord?" And he proceeded to tell the Lord all about Saul, as if the Lord did not already know. Ananias may not have had the faith to obey immediately, but he was on talking terms with the Lord. He was on good terms and was talking to the right person. He didn't leave and tell everyone in his church or on his prayer chain. He continued to speak to the Lord until he was clear about his instructions. Once he was clear, he did obey God, as faith came by hearing the word. There is nothing wrong with taking a word back to the Lord. He was getting his faith built up. He was getting some more information, and the Lord was happy to give it to him. There does come a point, however, of disobedience and unbelief. The Lord does not care for that (Heb. 10:38). When we receive a prophetic word, we have a responsibility to walk in it ourselves. To whom much is given, much is required. Obedience is a key to hearing from the Lord.

Proverbs 29:25 says, "*The fear of man brings a snare, but whoever trusts in the LORD shall be safe.*" Many times, the Lord will ask us to do things that do not appear safe. Ananias was stepping out on a limb to go locate Saul. He might have been thinking, "What if I get there and he is just pretending he is blind? And he has all his soldiers... this could be a ploy to capture me and throw me in prison. Is this the voice of the Lord, or is this some spirit that has been sent to get me out of hiding?" Many such things can go through our minds. But, Ananias knew the voice of the Lord, and he obeyed it, and great fruit came as a result of his obedience. We will be safe when we listen and obey the voice of the Lord. It may not seem that way at times, but we will be safe. We must obey.

4. Submission, One to Another

Looking again at the example of Simeon, here was a certain old man who listened to the Spirit. The Spirit had told him something very important: "You are not going to die until you see the Messiah." We do not know how long before the circumcision ceremony he was told this. Nevertheless, it must have been comforting to an old man to know that he would not die before he saw the Messiah. Then, by revelation, by the voice of God, he was summoned to the temple and began to speak the blessing over the Christ child. At that point, Anna the prophetess arrived. She did not come up to Simeon, push him out of the way and say, "Wait a minute. Where is your prophet card? Who gives you permission to speak those blessings? That's my job. I have been around for more than 100 years, and, by gosh, nobody is going to take that job away from me. I have waited all this time to do the blessing. Now get out of my way!" Absolutely not. She came in and glorified God. There was humility on her part to submit to another.

The prophetic person must have the courage and strength to stand alone if called to, but, at the same time, have humility and wisdom to understand the need for corporateness. It has been said that no man is an island. We are not designed to stand alone. It is God's purpose to bring people together in Christ. We need to submit one to another. Proper relationship is required, including discipleship, submission to authority, loyalty, and accountability. These all build character. God will not trust us with greater things unless we prove to Him our willingness to submit to the Spirit of Christ manifesting through someone else.

If someone receives a prophetic word, it needs to be submitted. There is probably not a ministry in the Body of Christ that needs to be mentored more constructively and shepherded more effectually—and with more compassion—than that of the prophetic. If the devil is allowed to come in and offend us and get us to speak things which are not of God, then he has authority to use our words for destructive purposes. Submission takes trust. Our trust needs to be in the Lord, but we also need to trust others who are of good character and who are submitted unto the Lord. If we will humble ourselves under the mighty hand of God, He will raise us up in due time.

Apostles and prophets need one another. Together they form the foundation of the Church (Eph. 2:20). As the understanding of corporateness increases, we will see more power exercised and more authority delegated to the prophets. Maturity in the prophetic produces the under-standing that we are a part of the Body, each needing the ministry of the other. This is why prophetic people, many times, feel left out of the Body because they have had to go through a maturing time in the wilderness. They may have come to the point of feeling like they can never fit in with the Body. Part of that results from sin in the Body of Christ when the voice of God is not allowed in the Church. By and large, the Church does not want to know what the prophets are seeing and hearing for fear of it being unset-tling. Because the vessel is imperfect, it may not look the way we think it should. The prophet must do everything possible for the word to be received, but if it is rejected, he or she must understand that it is the word being rejected, not the person delivering it. That is why we need to do all within our power to purify our character so the word is not rejected because of us.

5. Maturity

If you have a genuine call to function as a prophet, then just do the job and the people will come. Do not go out of your way to make yourself known as a prophet. First Kings 13 gives an account of a young man of God from Judah who prophesied against the altars in Bethel. With tremendous confirmation of his word, immediately the altar split and fire came down from heaven. Immediately, King Jeroboam pointed to him and ordered the soldiers to arrest him. As soon as he pointed at him, the king's hand withered up. The young man of God was prophesying the name of a king to be born 400 years later who would clean that place up. After Jeroboam's hand had withered, he asked the young man of God to pray for him. The man of God agreed, and the Lord healed Jeroboam immediately. Jeroboam offered him a gift, which was wisely declined because the Lord's instructions to the young man were to return without recompense. On the young man's way back, an old prophet, who really was not walking with the Lord (though it does not say he was a false prophet), came and found him. It appears the older prophet just wanted fellowship with this young man because he had heard of the manifestation of the power of God. The story ends as the young man of God loses his life because he submitted himself to illegitimate authority and disobeyed the instructions which the Lord had given him. The older prophet had said,

> *I too am a prophet as you are, and an angel spoke to me by the word of the LORD, saying, "Bring him back with you to your house, that he may eat bread and drink water"* (1 Kings 13:18b).

The young man allowed himself to be flattered and accepted the invitation to go to the old prophet's home, even though God had told him not to. The young man was clearly operating in prophetic authority, but he was still young. God had not given him the title of prophet yet because he was still maturing. The older prophet was lying to him. The young man allowed himself to be flattered, and this cost him his life and his ministry.

There is a lesson to be learned here. We need maturity. There is nothing wrong with being known as what you are called to be, but we do not need to grasp after it. A man's gift will make room for him. It is a mistake often made by the immature or anxious to try to make room for their gift. Ask yourself this question: "Do I want to *be* a prophet, or do I wish to be *known* as a prophet?" If the desire is to be known, it will usually lead to problems. Our directive is to be humble *"that He may exalt you in due time"* (1 Pet. 5:6). If we have any other motivation than to allow the Lord to exalt and acknowledge us in His time, than we are not yet ready to be revealed. Prophets must grow into their authority. Authority comes from revelation and responsibility. Revelation brings with it an authority or grace to bring the word to pass. Authority begins with revelation, which makes way for responsibility. With responsibility comes a need for accountability, which in turn puts us in a place to be trusted with more authority. Thus there is a progression of authority. I call this the "RARA" principle. Revelation leads to Accountability, which places us in a position of Responsibility, and with Responsibility comes Authority. There is an unfortunate presumption that revelation leads directly and immediately to authority. This misunderstanding has often caused tragic consequences. In fact, with revelation comes a responsibility to go to God to find out how to deliver it and when. It is the responsibility of the prophet to bring a word through love. This being done, others will see the fruit and entrust us with more authority.

6. Fear of Man

The fear of man is probably the root of almost every pitfall that is encountered in the prophetic. It may well be the root of all stumbling blocks in our Christian walk. There are two sides to the fear of man: one is the fear to speak because of rejection; the other is the desire to be recognized. Once, I heard Bob Jones say that God always calls the prophetic from deep rejection. I made a mental note that in Psalm 27:10, David said, *"When my father and my mother forsake me, then the LORD will take care of me."* David was also rejected. His father did not even have him summoned when Samuel came to anoint the future king of Israel. When Samuel asked if there were any other sons, Jesse apologetically mentioned another son in the field. He would not even bring him in for dinner (1 Sam. 16:11). This is how rejected David was by his own family. But, out of this rejection came a tremendous prophet, priest, and king.

A prophet will not, however, hear clearly from the Lord if there is a stronghold of rejection or fear of man. The fear of man brings confusion, which is like idolatry unto the Lord. When we fear men, we have placed men above God. The fear of man and the fear of rejection are broken by the power of a strong relationship with God. The wilderness experience gives us enduring strength to stand. Fasting alone will not replace the wilderness experience and knowing the hiding place of the Almighty. We need to know God face to face. Paul Cain says, "On earth we are known by the things we say, but in heaven we are known by the things we keep to ourselves." A prophet must have a strong relationship with the Lord, or else he will not go very far. In the face of rejection, a prophet must stay under the shadow of the Almighty and receive strength. He must go into that place of peace which does not come from his surroundings. Even in prison, he must sing praises to God. I have often had to counsel those who see prophetically but do not have a proper avenue for release. They are called only to pray. Unless they are freed from the need to be recognized by man and enabled to stand in the presence of the Lord and His revelations, they will not be able to keep the revelation between themselves and the Lord. This position is the cause of many frustrating situations for the individual and those to whom they attempt to deliver a message. Fear of man produces confusion, which leads to frustration, which leads to anger. Anger, like bitterness, will taint the message and can bring judgment to the prophet. There are too many prophetic men and women who have a burning anger because of rejection or past hurts. These things need to be healed before the individual can continue forward in the things of the Lord.

7. Worship

Jeremiah 7:2 says,

Stand in the gate of the Lord's house, and proclaim there this word, and say, "Hear the word of the LORD, all you of Judah who enter in at these gates to worship the LORD"!

There are many instances in the Word of God where worship and prophecy are found together. Most of the

Psalms were songs that were sung prophetically and written down. Many of these are still sung in Hebrew circles today. They know the melodies which accompany those psalms. They were prophesied in song in the company of the musicians. Elisha called for the musician when the king asked for him to bring a word (2 Kings 3:15). Worshipful music creates an atmosphere of peace and joy whereby the Word of the Lord can be received. Worship will lead to and increase the prophetic anointing. God chooses to manifest Himself through our praises and worship.

8. Intercession

Intercession is prayer in action. When Moses stood on the mountain above the battle with Amalek and held his arms up, Israel was winning. Aaron and Hur came and held his arms up as he grew tired. This was intercession (Exod. 17). But, as far as the account states, there was no prayer offered. Prophetic acts will release angels into battle when the actions are in agreement with the Holy Spirit. There are numerous good books written on the subject of intercession. Here, I simply desire to identify intercession as an attribute of prophetic character. Once, Dr. C. Peter Wagner raised the question to me of where to draw the line between intercessor and prophet. I had to admit it is not always a clear line. But, for definition, I will state that while most intercessors may be prophetic, *ALL* prophets must be intercessors. Intercession may actually be a major entrance into the prophetic for many people, but a prophet will always remain an intercessor. The calling as intercessor will continue to adapt and change according to the call of God upon his or her life and the requirements of his or her ministry.

9. The Speaking of Blessings

In Luke 2:34, it says that Simeon blessed Mary and the infant Jesus. At first glance, his words do not sound like much of a blessing. Simeon prophesied that the Child was destined for the "fall and rising of many in Israel." He prophesied Jesus would be spoken against. He added that a sword would pierce through Mary's own soul. I do not consider these especially "fun" words. Wouldn't you want to get your money back from that 900 number if you called expecting good news? Yet, it says, "He spoke blessings." Those were blessings because they were from God. It was information Mary kept and pondered in her heart. The words ministered to her years later even though they were hard words to hear. If a prophet brings a hard word, it must be done in humility and love.

I believe there is a further distinction between a message brought through a person standing in the office of a prophet and a prophetic word of simple prophecy. Words brought through a prophetic person must fit into the category set by the Holy Spirit through the apostle Paul in 1 Corinthians 14:3: *"But he who prophesies speaks edification and exhortation and comfort to men."* A word given through the simple empowerment of prophecy must fit into one or more of these categories if it is to be proper according to Scripture, especially when delivered within the context of the Church. A prophet, on the other hand, must speak the word of the Lord regardless of content. Often, it may contain direction and possibly even reproof or correction.

There will be blessings which are attained if the correction is heeded, but the message may not seem so edifying when it is first delivered. There is a big difference between the word delivered through the office of a prophet and the simple empowerment of prophecy. There is a higher level of responsibility and a higher level of accountability. To go from one into the second improperly can lead to problems, and many are led astray unknowingly. If we move by our own motivation from the simple gift of prophecy, which is always edification and exhortation and comfort, into the office of a prophet, we will end up discouraged and confused, as will many others.

It is possible to bring a word of exhortation, which is also restoration, as the Lord reveals something out of order. Galatians 6:1 says that when a brother is caught in a fault, we are to restore him in a spirit of meekness. As the Lord reveals this, our response should be to intercede for the person or take the person aside and talk to him privately. It must be done in a spirit of meekness and restoration, not reproof. Part of the word may be reproof, but the discipline is closely related to the relationship you have with the person. If you have no relationship with him or her, then it may be better to pray and not confront. If we will have this attitude, the Church will receive the prophet and look forward to correction and reproof.

10. Prophets Are Servants to God and to Mankind

Gifting does not insure character. The gifts are received by faith, but fruit comes through character. Fruit is drawn out through service to others. There is an old saying that

"God desires spiritual fruit, not religious nuts." The Lord said we can judge prophets by fruit, not by giftings (Matt. 7:16). There are many false prophets that have great power and gifts in operation, *but the fruit is lacking.* In a sense, the young man of God in 1 Kings 13 fell into that trap. He followed after a gift where there was no fruit.

11. Be Just and Devout

We have to be just and devout because Jesus promised that we will suffer for His sake if we obey Him. Jesus was perfect, and yet they found reason to kill Him for blasphemy. The accuser will come. Just make sure he has no true ammunition, *"giving no offense in any thing, that the ministry be not blamed"* (2 Cor. 6:3). I like to say that if we live for the Lord, accusations will come—our only responsibility is to be sure the accusations are false. If we do that, then we can boldly say,

> *No weapon formed against me shall prosper, and every tongue which rises against me in judgment I shall condemn. This is the heritage of the servants of the LORD, and their righteousness is from Me* (Isa. 54:17).

12. Proper Timing

When we receive a word, we are required to discover His timing. The prophet may ask the Lord, "Do you even want me to deliver this, or is this just something between you and me that I need to pray about? Do you only want me to intercede?" Jesus knew that Lazarus was sick and that he would die. Others encouraged Jesus to go to Lazarus immediately and pray for his healing. But, Jesus knew the need to be obedient to the Father for timing.

When Jesus did arrive, He was able to pray,

> *Father, I thank You that You have heard Me. And I know that You always hear Me, but because of the people who are standing by I said this, that they may believe that You sent Me* (John 11:41,42).

And then He cried out prophetically, "Lazarus, come forth!"

Chapter 4

Receiving a Prophetic Word and Delivering a Prophetic Word

I N JAMES 4:2, IT SAYS, *"You have not because you ask not."* We need to go to God to receive from Him. If we will ask for a word from God, He will give it if He has one for us. This is especially true as we become more trustworthy to accomplish what He would like done. First Corinthians 14:1 says, *"Pursue love and desire spiritual gifts, but especially that you may prophesy...."* The word *desire* is the Greek word *zello,* from which we get our word *zealous.* We need to be zealous after spiritual gifts. In Jeremiah 23:30, it says, *"'Therefore behold I am against the prophets,' says the Lord, 'Who steal My words every one from his neighbor.'"* Did you know words from the Lord can be stolen? The prophets steal the words, every one, from their neighbor by repetition. However, it is not always wrong to repeat a word. Anna repeated Simeon's words to everyone. The difference between what Anna did and Jeremiah's warning is the motive behind the repetition.

Learn to hear His voice. His voice always brings redemption. The accuser brings condemnation. Often, a word carries both because we have this treasure in earthen vessels. Our souls are the clearinghouse for prophecy, and our souls are impure. First Corinthians 14:32 says the spirit of the prophets is subject to the prophets. Anything received from heaven comes to our spirit, but then has to go through our soul—our minds being in this category—before being released. This is why it is so important to control our souls by renewing our minds and leading every thought captive to Christ.

Without consistency and discipline, there will be no dependability or reliability. Those who say, "Thus says the Lord" when He did not, are undisciplined at best. The phrase "the Lord told me" is over used by those who are young in the prophetic. In Jeremiah 23:31,32, it says,

> *"Behold, I am against the prophets," says the LORD, "who use their tongues and say, 'He says.' Behold, I am against those who prophesy false dreams," says the LORD, "and tell them, and cause My people to err by their lies and by their recklessness. Yet I did not send them or command them; therefore they shall not profit this people at all," says the LORD.*

Zeal can never replace wisdom, but zeal will keep the mature young at heart. In delivering a prophetic word, it is possible to have the correct attitude but the wrong application. This is also remedied by discipline. A received word must be applied accurately. If I get a word for one person and I give it to that person, but then I go ahead and give it to another also, is it a true word? No, not for the second person. By giving it to the second person, there is a possibility that I could cause it to become a false word even to the original recipient.

To administer a sure word of prophecy, say only what the Father said. Protect yourself and others from control and witchcraft. Witchcraft is soulish manipulation by words or actions. In John 5:19, Jesus said, *"The Son can do nothing of Himself, but what He sees the Father do; for whatever He does, the Son also does in like manner."*

The sons of the prophets are a biblical model. They did not have to worry about getting stoned because they just went in and did the best they could, knowing they were under the mentorship of Samuel, Elijah, or whoever it was to whom they were submitted. This is not seen often enough in the Body of Christ today. The first place where we need to judge prophecy is within our hearts, in our spirits. Is there a big check within us, or is there, what I describe as, a green light. I would describe a check in my spirit as a feeling similar to a knot in my stomach—only it is not physical. We can have peace within ourselves even if we do not understand a word. Or, we can have a check even if the word appears to make perfect sense to us. We need to be able to listen to our hearts accurately because the Spirit of God dwells there.

There are different components of revelation. Any prophecy or prophetic word has three parts to it. **The first part is the revelation, dream, or vision itself. The second is the interpretation**, answering the question "What does the revelation mean?" The interpretation can come in increments over a period of time. And, **the third part is the application**. It can be immediate, or it can be long term. In regard to dreams or visions, God might use dark sayings, or He may show us plainly face to face. In Numbers 12:6-8, God said,

> *Hear now My words: If there is a prophet among you, I, the LORD, make Myself known to him in a vision; I speak to him in a dream. Not so with My servant Moses; He is faithful in all My house. I speak with him face to face, even plainly, and not in dark sayings; And he sees the form of the LORD. Why then were you not afraid to speak against My servant Moses?*

There are different levels, different ways that God speaks. He spoke to Moses face to face. Although we "see through a glass darkly," if we will submit ourselves to those dreams and visions and dark sayings, if we will pursue God, He will reveal their meaning to us. He wants us to come to Him for the interpretation. He wants us to come to Him for the information. He wants us to come to Him for the application. He wants us to be dependent upon Him.

A word of knowledge or a prophecy can change a life. None of us will ever prophesy all things or have all knowledge. It will not happen. We know in part, and we prophesy in part (1 Cor. 13:9). We are a body. He will give one of us a part, and then He will give a part to another. He wants us depending upon Him. As we train ourselves to come back to Him, we will begin to see God more and more face to face.

How does He talk to you? Different than how He talks to me because we are individuals. He speaks to you in a language that you understand, one that touches your heart. In Isaiah 30:21, it says,

> *Your ears shall hear a word behind you, saying, "This is the way, walk in it, whenever you turn to the right hand or whenever you turn to the left."*

Mostly, He directs us by His peaceful voice that says, "This is the way." In Jeremiah 32:6, Jeremiah said, *"The word* of *the LORD came* to *me, saying…"* (it told him what to do, and he carried it out). Then in verse 8, he said, *"and then I knew that this was the Word* of *the Lord."* Jeremiah received the word and was obedient to carry it out and believe it. But, only after he obeyed did he know it was the Lord. If Jeremiah sometimes was not clear until after he had obeyed, what about us?

God spoke to Moses and said for him to go down to Egypt and tell Pharaoh to let His people go. The Lord also told Moses that He would do many miracles. Moses asked for a sign to know if these things were true. God said, "After you go down there and all these miracles happen, Pharaoh will resist you, but he will eventually let the people go. You are going to bring them back here, and you are going to worship Me on this mountain. Then you will know it was Me" (Exod. 3:12). That was his sign. Go do it. When you come back, that will be the sign. This is not the kind of sign we like, is it? However, this is often God's way. He expects us to walk in faith and rewards us for doing that. Confirmation is according to His will, and if we always require confirmation before obeying, we will one day find ourselves missing God. The Lord once spoke to me, "You do not need to understand in order to obey. If you wait until you understand before obeying, you will remain behind while others go forward." God will always confirm His word, often by the fruit it produces after it is carried out and not before.

I like to describe understanding as the louvers in a blind. From one angle, you cannot see out. As you change your position, the view becomes unobstructed. From the new angle, you can look outside and see everything clearly. What has changed? Nothing but your position. When we go out in faith, we have changed our position. We can receive from the Lord, and we can say, like Jeremiah did, "Now I know it is the Lord." Biblically, there are three Hebrew words that are translated as "a prophet" or "a seer." There is *roeh*, which is a seer, someone who sees open visions and is also able to interpret them. That same word is used for someone who sees with natural eyes and understands. This level of prophet sees in the spirit with deeper understanding. There are not that many prophets in the Scriptures who see open visions in proportion to the other types listed.

Then, there is *chozeh*. The meaning of this word emphasizes spiritual apprehension of internal visions. The word *chozeh* is translated as prophet or seer, but appears to be subordinate to the *roeh* type of seer because of the authority that comes through understanding. I believe that this view is contained in Isaiah 29:10:

> For the LORD has poured out on you the spirit of deep sleep, and has closed your eyes, namely, the prophets (chozeh); And He has covered your heads, namely, the seers (roeh).

Those considered seers in the higher sense, *roeh*, are usually given a preeminence over the other types of prophets. Samuel, a *roeh* type of seer, was regarded above other prophets and seers of his day, as he was not only a prophet sent with a message, but often had a deeper understanding and insight to go along with the vision he carried. He was a leader of leaders. Daniel was esteemed above all the other prophets and wise men of his time because of the understanding which accompanied his prophetic gifts. Daniel 1:17 says,

> *As for these four children, God gave them knowledge and skill in all learning and wisdom: and Daniel had understanding in all visions and dreams.*

Seers have visions. When God spoke to Jeremiah, who was a seer, He asked him, *"Jeremiah, what do you see?"* Jeremiah said, *"I see a branch of an almond tree"* (Jer. 1:11). God did not ask Jeremiah, "What do you feel?" or "What do you think?" What do you *see* is a question for a seer. Jesus also was a seer.

> *Nathanael said to Him, "How do You know me?" Jesus answered and said to him, "Before Philip called you, when you were under the fig tree, I saw you* (John 1:48).

And He said to them, *"I saw Satan fall like lightning from heaven"* (Luke 10:18).

Lastly, there is the Hebrew word *nabiy*, which is the most common biblical word used for the prophetic. It describes someone who has the Spirit working within him. It is a word for inspiration. Every prophet receives this type of inspiration, and in the New Testament, all believers can and should operate at this level at least in its elementary levels. Every prophet will be the *nabiy* kind, but not every prophet will be the *roeh* kind. First Chronicles 29:29 contains all three of these Hebrew words:

> *Now the acts of King David, first and last, indeed they are written in the book of Samuel the seer (roeh), in the book of Nathan the prophet (nabiy), and in the book of Gad the seer (chozeh).*

Any given prophet will have different long suits in regard to these three types of inspiration. Some will see open visions, some will have angelic visitations, some dreams, visions and trances, and some or all will have inspirations and leadings of the inner witness. Those who walk with authority in the empowerment of words of knowledge usually fall into the category of a *chozeh* prophet or seer. Those who walk powerfully in words of wisdom generally fall into the category of the *roeh* prophet or seer, many times operating as a prophet to prophets because of the wisdom and understanding which is manifested through this type of ministry. All who walk in the prophetic must learn *nabiy* inspiration. This is generally the first type that we should become proficient with. I like to call this category of the prophetic the still small voice.

Chapter 5

Twelve Expressions of Inspiration

THERE ARE A NUMBER of different means by which the Lord can and does communicate with us, and while He does not change, He does deal with us as individuals. The Lord communicates with all of His children, but because many are not aware of how He communicates, it is possible to miss receiving the information or to not recognize the source of the information received. I have found that by simply identifying the means that the Spirit employs to communicate with us, people often have been able to more readily identify the voice of the Lord in their lives. In this chapter, I want to look at twelve different means, which I have identified, that the Spirit of the Lord uses to communicate His will to us.

1. Impressions

An impression is like a feeling or intuition. Often, I get the sense that the Spirit is pressing upon me in a certain way. This is a form of discernment. The still small voice really is under this category. In Numbers 11:29, Moses said to Joshua,

> *Are you zealous (or envious or upset) for my sake? Oh, that all the Lord's people were prophets and that the Lord would put His Spirit upon them!*

Nabiy is the Hebrew word used here for prophets. Everyone who is born again is in this category now. Paul said we all may prophesy. This is exactly what he meant. We are all in that category as far as we can receive through inspiration and receive through the voice of God and then speak His words.

2. A Knowing or Witness

Romans 9:1 says, *"I tell the truth in Christ, I am not lying, my conscience also bearing me witness in the Holy Spirit."* We all have an inner witness. It is called Christ in you. It is the mind of Christ that tells us what we ought to do or ought not to do. First John 5:10 says, *"He who believes in the Son of God has a witness in himself."* All believers have this. If we have confessed Jesus as Lord, we have an inner witness that is ours that will lead us in the way that we should go. The Spirit may witness within our spirit information about another individual or situation which we would have no way of knowing in our senses. Take action, in love, upon these witnesses of the Spirit. This is often how we initially enter the realm of *word of knowledge, word of wisdom*, and *discerning of spirits.*

3. We Can Feel Things

We can receive things in the emotions of our soul and in our bodies. This is why it is so important to sanctify ourselves. First Peter 3:15 says,

> But sanctify the Lord God in your hearts and always be ready to give a defense of everyone who asks you the reason of the hope that is in you with meekness and fear.

The word does not come through your flesh, but the word can effect the flesh. Often, I have had the sense that the Spirit is touching a part of my body in order to communicate a message to me. There may be other times, however, when one might say, "Well, I just felt it was God" and it was not God at all. It was the lusts that are in our flesh, and we ascribed it to Him. It is important to allow ourselves room to grow. If we have the attitude that we cannot be wrong in our interpretations or feel the need to always say, "God told me," then we will hinder our ability to mature. This is why we need to be mentored and to submit ourselves and what we are receiving to other proven people who are committed to assisting us in our growth.

4. Visions

The first and most common manifestations of visions are visions of the spirit in the heart. The eyes can be open or closed. Seeing a vision and interpreting what is being seen are not one and the same. The prophet Daniel, one of Scriptures' greatest seers, often had to seek the Lord for long periods of time to receive the understanding of a vision. Interpretations belong to the Lord, as Joseph stated while still in the Egyptian prison.

5. Supernatural Senses

In this level, the five senses are amplified in sensitivity and ability. One can experience "x-ray vision" to see through something or a heightened sense of smell or hearing. A "foul spirit" may be discerned through spiritual smell. One may hear across a distance a sound of conversation which could not be heard with normal physical senses. Once, while I was waiting between flights in a European airport, I overheard something which caught my interest as one man spoke to another. However, at the time, the two men were on the other side of a very crowded and noisy restaurant and impossible to be heard naturally from where I was. It was as if the volume of those few words were increased and then the volume was returned to normal. I remember recognizing immediately that the Spirit must want me to meet these men. I took the opportunity to walk over and introduce myself. The men turned out to be ministers returning home to America. As we spoke, I received important information from them which soon was to impact many leaders in my ministry.

It is also possible that a taste will communicate something spiritual to you. There is a record in the Old Testament of Elisha's prophets in training making up some porridge and tasting "death in the pot" (2 Kings 4:40). How did they know there was death in the pot? Nobody had died. God communicated supernaturally through their sense of taste.

6. Dreams

The next level is dreams. They are seen all through the Bible. At Bethel, Jacob saw angels go up and down a ladder. Joseph saw a vision or dream of the moon and the stars. He dreamed of the sheaves bowing down and got himself in big trouble by telling his family about it.

> *In a dream, in a vision of the night, when deep sleep falls upon men, while slumbering on their beds, then He opens the ears of men, and seals their instruction. In order to turn man from his deed, and conceal pride from man* (Job 33:15-17).

God will often use dreams to communicate warnings and other important information to us in order to avoid as much interference from our senses as possible.

7. Open Visions

This is where the eyes are open and one sees spiritual things as though they appeared normal to the natural eyes. It is possible for the open vision to be so real to our eyes that it is only later understood that it was an open vision. It is likewise possible to actually be involved in the physical sense in a spiritual phenomenon only to realize later that it was not a vision. This happened to Peter in Acts 12:11.

8. Trances

This manifestation is distinct from visions because in a vision, one is still aware of one's surroundings. In a trance, the surroundings are blotted out temporarily, unless God wants them to be observed. This also occurred to Peter in Acts 10.

9. Audible Voices

Acts 9 is the account of Paul's encounter with the Lord while traveling to Damascus. He was knocked to the ground, and a conversation occurred between him and the Lord. In verse 7, it says the other men stood by and heard a voice, but they did not see anyone. To Paul, it was an audible voice. In my experience, the audible voice of God will always be life changing, no matter the length or brevity of the conversation.

10. Visitations from Angels

Angels can bring us information. An angel came to Daniel to bring him understanding. Angels came to Abraham because there was something important that needed to happen that he needed to be informed about. Mary spoke with the angel Gabriel, the same archangel who communicated to Daniel. Joseph was ministered to by an angel through a dream, as was Jacob.

11. Visitations from the Lord

At times, there may be a commissioning that the Lord Jesus Himself will administer. It is often difficult for the person to communicate what happened in human words. It may not be something they want people to know about, especially since many people would not believe it. The Lord may come at other times, and He said that He would manifest Himself to those who love Him (John 14:21).

12. Translation in Place or Time

Both Paul and John were caught up into the third heaven. They were experienced in doing service for the Body of Christ, in bringing the word of God so that the Body would prosper. Preparation could then be made for the things that were ahead. When we have a servant's heart like that and are willing to give our lives as living sacrifices, then we will grow up in all things unto Him who is the Head. We will grow up to the place where we can see Him face to face like Moses did and be able to receive that sure word of prophecy which will change lives and change the nations as they are given the prophetic word.

Philip was caught up by the Spirit and physically translated from the desert of Gaza to Azotus (Acts 8). On the Mount of transfiguration, four men—that is Jesus, Peter, James, and John—were translated to a future time where they saw the Lord standing in His glorified and resurrected body with Moses and Elijah. There is no record in Scripture of more than one person sharing an internal vision simultaneously with another. I believe that in this case, all were translated to a time after Jesus's resurrection. Enoch, as well as Elijah, were translated to be with the Lord and are examples of those who were physically translated into the heavenly realm of eternity.

Chapter 6

Interpretation of Visions and Dreams

A LL SCRIPTURE IS prophecy (2 Pet. 1:21). We know in part, and we prophesy in part (1 Cor. 13:9). No prophet can interpret apart from the Holy Spirit. God intends for us to know the part that we need, the part that will change our lives, and put it on track or keep it on track. It is usually not that difficult upon seeing a vision to describe what has been seen. The difficulty often comes when deciphering the meaning. There are times when the Lord will simply tell what it means, as He did for Jeremiah.

> *Moreover the word of the LORD came to me, saying, "Jeremiah, what do you see?" And I said, "I see a branch of an almond tree." Then the LORD said to me, "You have seen well, for I am ready to perform My word."*

And the word of the LORD came to me the second time, saying, "What do you see?" And I said, "I see a boiling pot, and it is facing away from the north." Then the LORD said to me: "Out of the north calamity shall break forth on all the inhabitants of the land. For behold, I am calling all the families of the kingdoms of the north," says the LORD; "They shall come and each one set his throne at the entrance of the gates of Jerusalem, against all its walls all around, and against all the cities of Judah" (Jer. 1:11-15).

The Lord gave visions to Jeremiah and, in these two cases, explained to him what He was saying through the visions. Generally speaking, however, when a vision or dream is received, an interpretation is necessary. This is where we must be extremely cautious not to get off track. This is in part because we receive the prophetic through a human filter.

Interpretation simply means "understanding." Often, what is called a false prophecy is not a false prophecy at all. It is just a wrong interpretation. As a prophet gives the interpretation, again, he needs to be humble and meek. Do not say, "Thus says the Lord" if it is not so. It is okay to say, "It seems to me what the Lord is saying is such and such. Take it back to the Lord and see." The vision or the revelation itself can be described with authority, but unless the Lord also gives the application with equal authority and clarity, we need to be humble and say as much. Integrity and an honest character will affect the way people receive the prophetic that we so desperately need in the Church today. An interpretation need not be given by one person alone. We are the body of Christ. Together, we, not you or me alone, have the mind of Christ. We can come together to interpret and seek the Lord to find out what God is saying through a word, a dream, a vision, or a revelation. Please do not misunderstand. I am not suggesting a committee to bring interpretations. Committees do not receive revelation, but we each may receive "a part," which together will confirm what message the Lord is speaking.

Many times, God will give a dream or a vision in the night. *"Then He opens the ears of men, and seals their instruction. In order to turn man from his deed, and conceal pride from man"* (Job 33:16,17). When we are asleep, there is less of our souls to interfere with God giving us the word. One may wonder if a dream was indeed from God. Or, one may wake up in the middle of the night and ponder the dream for awhile, but by morning it cannot be remembered. It is good to keep a notebook or tape recorder by your bed. If we will be faithful to write our dreams down, God will speak more often. Once, C. Peter Wagner encouraged me to write out the prophetic words which I had received. Up until that point, I had simply saved the cassette recordings of words which I had received and occasionally, I might replay one or another of them. It is quite amazing how often God has spoken a word through someone since I began to keep a written record of the words God has intended for me. If we will take the word of the Lord seriously, He will give it to us more earnestly. Rick Joyner tells a story about seeking the Lord and why he was not receiving more visions. It turned out he had not been getting any visions for quite a few months. The Lord said, "Why should I? You do not take them seriously. You do not write them down." If God gives them, there is a specific purpose for them. Do not treat them lightly. Man lives by every *rhema* word that proceeds out of the mouth of God. We are responsible to take them seriously if He is going to give them. So, keep a pen and paper nearby and write them down—even if you do not know what they mean at the time. It may be months or years before the interpretation comes, but the interpretation will come in God's timing.

The main way to check prophecy and interpretation is through the Scriptures and by knowing the heart of God. Second Peter 1:19 says, *"And so we have the prophetic word confirmed."* The King James version calls it *"the more sure word of prophecy."* We have the prophetic word confirmed through Scripture. Genesis 40:8 states, *"Interpretations belong to God."* Many give little thought to the visions experienced during the day and short dreams we receive as being from God. We need to take them seriously. Many times, He gives them to see what you will do with them. *"He who is faithful in the least can be faithful in much"* (Luke 16:10). We should not expect to get a book-long version of a dream or a vision right off the bat. Be faithful with the little ones. Those little ones can be life changing. It is some of those little ones that have set men of God into ministries that have changed the world and the course of history. The word *"This is My beloved Son in whom I am well pleased"* (Matt. 3:17) was not a very long word, but it was a powerful one. *"This is My beloved Son, in whom I am well pleased. Hear Him!"* (Matt. 17:5) is another.

God can often reveal much more to us through the process of interpretation than if He spoke His meaning straightforwardly. In the process of going through the interpretation, many times, we come closer to God. He becomes magnified in our hearts as we see the wonder of what He has done and how He has done it. When we see something in the form of a vision or a dream, often, much more information can be given in a shorter amount of time then verbiage could communicate in the same space of time. A picture is worth a thousand words.

Jesus said over and over again, "He that has ears to hear let him hear!" Pray this prayer to Him: "Lord, I want to be one who hears. I want to be one who hears what the Spirit is saying to the Church." The word *hear* in the Greek is to hear not so much rationally as to hear and understand. Jesus spoke in obscure parables to separate those people who wanted to receive from those who were willing to give in order to receive. The latter were the ones who were truly seeking the Kingdom of God. To those willing to give in order to receive the Lord says, "I will give you the keys to the Kingdom." Keys unlock things. They unravel obscure sayings and dreams. The Spirit is the source of these keys—not formulas. Americans, especially, often want the formula for success, the formula for faith, the formula for raising the dead, the formula for prosperity. We are looking for a recipe book when the Lord wants us to learn directly from the Master Chef.

Let us look now at some examples in the Bible of visions and dreams and how they can be interpreted.

Moreover the word of the Lord came to me, saying, "Jeremiah, what do you see?" And I said, "I see a branch of an almond tree." Then the Lord said to me, "You have

71

seen well, for I am ready to perform My word" (Jer. 1:11,12).

The almond tree is one of the first trees to bud in the spring. So, its appearance indicates the commencement of springtime. This was to be understood as "something is beginning." The Lord said, "Yes, you have seen that correctly, and I am ready to perform My word." Thus, the fulfillment of the promise is beginning to happen now. This is one way to interpret this vision. But, there is more to it. In the Hebrew language, there is a play on words here. It is a rhyme. The word *almond* is *shaqad* (long "a" sound), and the word *ready* is *shaqad* (an "aw" sound).

God said, "What do you see?"

Jeremiah said, "I see the rod of a *shaqad* tree."

God said, "That is correct, and I am ready to perform, *shaqad*, My word."

Thus, God gave Jeremiah, in the form of a word picture, a double confirmation that He would perform His word. Images of the mind stick with us much more tenaciously and possess much more force than words and thoughts alone. There is a key to interpretation in this passage. The Lord said, "What do you see?" and Jeremiah said, "This is what I see." Notice He did not say, "What do you think that means?" God told him what it meant, but the conversation started with, "What do you see?" This is where we should start—not with what we think it means, but with what we actually see. There will be times, however, when a direct communication of the message and not the vision itself should be given. But, for the most part, it is most prudent to say what was seen.

SYMBOLS

The following are some examples of interpretation, including many symbols from the Bible. I consider them to be fairly reliable, but interpretations are not to be limited to the examples given. Allow the Holy Spirit to teach and guide you as He extends your borders.

1. A lampstand or a candlestick can represent the spirit or the lamp of the church, as in the book of Revelation (Rev. 1:20).

2. A rock can represent something that is solid, something that is heavy. It can represent a foundation, something immovable, something that is stable. It can represent Jesus or *living stones*, which are the people of the Church who are being built together (Eph. 2:22, 1 Pet. 2:5).

3. Sheep can represent simply sheep, but generally, they represent people. We are the sheep of His pasture. Jesus is our Shepherd.

4. A star may represent an angel or a messenger. It could represent the Morning Star, Jesus. In Revelation, the seven stars are messengers to the churches (Rev. 1:20).

5. Hair can represent strength. It can represent glory. It can represent wisdom. All those things are seen in the Bible. Gray hair or long hair specifically speaks of wisdom or glory.

6. Age also speaks of wisdom.

7. Teeth speak of relationship. Teeth are like pairs of sheep. Teeth come in pairs, so teeth speak of a relationship between people. Proverbs 25:19 says, *"Confidence in an unfaithful man in time of trouble is like a bad tooth or a foot out of joint."* I know a number of situations where people have had major toothaches, and the root of it was not a physical toothache at all. The feeling was the result of a relationship they had come into which had brought a curse. When the curse was broken, the toothache immediately left.

8. Oil represents the anointing. It can represent the Holy Spirit. It can represent blessings which are passed down. An example is the oil upon Aaron's head in Psalm 133:1.

9. Water can represent blessings or abundance. It can represent people. It can represent the spiritual realm. The book of Revelation states, *"I heard the sounds of many waters...."* These "waters" were people from many nations.

10. Fish can represent people, life, or activity, as in Matthew 13.

11. A king or a queen can represent a nation or authority. They represent the headship that is in authority.

12. A horse can represent speed or transportation to a place. Many times, horses speak of ministry. With a saddle upon it, the horse would be a prepared or functioning ministry.

13. Feet of flint speak of sparks flying. The fire can speak of the Holy Spirit or importance: *"...how great a matter a little fire kindles."*

14. Vehicles can speak of various types of ministry or businesses. A car speaks of a family ministry or small ministry. A truck can represent a larger ministry. A plane can represent an international ministry. Ministries can be spoken of in terms of a field. Paul talked in terms of not going outside of his calling or his field, which was his sphere of authority as conferred upon him by the Lord.

15. Prisons can represent chains, bars, captives, and enslavement.

16. A hook can represent a snare or a stronghold. It can be God trying to tug on you. The Bible speaks of, *"putting a hook in the jaw."* When a king of old conquered another king, he would put a hook in the jaw of the captured king and parade him around to show his victory to the people. Hooks can represent a snare, a captive, or something to deter.

17. A shoulder can represent authority or responsibility. In Isaiah 9:6, it says, *"...and the government will be upon His shoulder."*

18. A saddle can represent a position, a job, or a call to ministry.

19. A camel can represent a burden bearer or a strength to go through a dry time and come through it all right.

20. Sparrows or swallows flocking around may represent curses. Proverbs 26:2 says, *"Like a flitting sparrow or a flying swallow so a curse without cause shall not alight."* These birds were wanting to find a place to land, but could not.

21. A rod, a staff, or a goad. Jesus said to Paul, *"Is it not difficult to kick against the goads?"* A goad was a rod with a pointed end that was used to keep the ox in the furrow while plowing. These can all represent authority. Paul was going against the authority of God.

22. An eye can represent understanding. Isaiah 20:9,10 says, *"For the Lord has poured out on you the spirit of deep sleep and has closed your eyes, namely the prophets."* The eye can represent prophetic understanding, but in general, it represents understanding.

23. A head or the top of a head can represent a leader; it can represent authority. Ezekiel 1:10 is part of a vision:

> *As for the likeness of their faces, each had the face of a man; each of the four had the face of a lion on the right side, each of the four had the face of an ox on the left side, and each of the four had the face of an eagle.*

Described here is the face of a man, a lion, an ox, and an eagle. Each of these represents different things.

a. The face of a man can represent Jesus, the Son of man, or a son of man. It also can represent the book of Luke which speaks of Jesus as the Son of man.

b. The lion is the king of beasts and can represent the king or a king. But, it also represents the book of Matthew, which gives the genealogy of Jesus, addressing His Jewish heritage and lineage to being the Messiah.

c. The ox speaks of strength, of the servant, and of the ministry of Jesus, which is the ministry of a servant. The book of Mark gives no genealogy of Jesus because, in those days, servants had no genealogy considered worth mentioning. The book of Mark shows Jesus as a servant. Interestingly, in the book of Mark, more demonic deliverances are recorded than all the other books combined. This indicates that, as servants of God, servants take authority over the devil on behalf of the master of the house. Thus, the ox represents Jesus doing the work.

d. The eagle represents the Son of God. It can also represent revelation or the heavenly realm. It also represents the book of John. John describes Jesus as the Son of God more often than all the other gospel writers.

24. A house may represent a family or lineage.

25. The right hand can represent blessings. In the East, the right hand is the hand of blessing. Jesus went to heaven and sat down at the right hand of God.

26. The left hand can be the hand of cursing, but it also can represent the grace to accomplish a task or the object of grace.

27. Colors:

Red can represent warfare. It can represent redemption. It can represent sacrifice.

Blue can represent revelation, the heavenly realm, or the spiritual realm.

Purple represents priesthood, kingship, or royalty.

Amber can represent revelation and visions or warfare in the heavenly realm.

White represents holiness and purity.

28. Cultural examples:

An elephant or tiger may represent India.

Horses can represent Tennessee or Kentucky. They could even represent the Kentucky derby itself.

A kangaroo may represent Australia.

A Kiwi bird might represent New Zealand.

A lei of flowers or perhaps a hula dancer may represent Hawaii.

29. Numbers in Scripture:

The number one means beginning. It can mean unity. We are one. Jesus said, *"I and the Father are one."* We become one flesh in marriage.

The number two can represent agreement or confirmation. When Pharaoh had the dream twice, Joseph said, *"The dream is one dream and it has been given to you twice because it is established."* The word established used there is the word *confirmed*. It is confirmed because it happened twice. It can also mean division: "di-vision" = two visions.

The number three represents completeness. It represents solid, substantial, divine protection. The spirit, soul, and body together constitute a complete person. Past, present, and future: this is the completeness of time. Animal, vegetable, and mineral: this represents the completeness of the things of the world. Father, Son, and Spirit: the completeness of the Godhead.

The number four can represent a trial. It is the world number. Earth, air, fire, water are the four elements. North, south, east, west are the four directions. Spring, summer, fall, winter are the four seasons. It is an earthly number. It is not necessarily evil simply because it is of the earth. It can be influenced by God, man, or evil.

The number five is the number for grace, favor, or reward. There are five gift ministries to the Church. Five crowns of the believer in heaven.

The number six is man's number. It can represent imperfection. It represents man because man was created on the sixth day. It can also represent work because men have to toil by the sweat of their brow, and even God Himself worked until the end of the sixth day. The number of the man who will be the Antichrist will be 666.

The number seven represents spiritual order or spiritual perfection. It is three plus four which is the completeness of the Spirit placed into the number for the world, the number four, to bring spiritual perfection to us. There are seven "ones" listed in Ephesians 4. There are seven Church epistles, Romans through Thessalonians, each representing spiritual perfection.

The number eight represents a new beginning, a new thing. The eighth day of the week is also the first day of the week. It is a new beginning.

The number nine represents conclusion or finality. It

can also represent a contest or battle. It can represent judgment. It is the number for the Holy Spirit: there are nine empowerments of the Holy Spirit, and there are nine fruit of the Holy Spirit.

The number ten represents order—ordinal perfection and numerical order—as well as a completed cycle.

The number eleven represents disorder, but it also represents things that are in progress. It can represent impending judgment—for instance, "It is the eleventh hour." It can also represent the prophetic. The prophetic needs to be mentored so it can bring order. Its purpose is to complete the cycle. When the prophetic word is in operation, we are in the eleventh hour, the time is almost up. But, we do not want the cycle to stop. We want to get to the twelfth stroke of the clock with everything we need. Eleven is a bridge between ten and twelve.

The number twelve is the number for governmental order, governmental perfection, rule, or judgment. Jesus had twelve apostles. There were twelve tribes in Israel. There are twelve legions of angels Jesus could have called. There were twelve judges in the Old Testament.

The number thirteen, by the Law of First Mention in Genesis 14:4, represents rebellion. It says, *"Twelve years they served and the thirteenth year they rebelled."* In US history, there were thirteen colonies that revolted against England.

Thirteen can signify rebellion and revolution. Many times in our culture, it has come to mean witchcraft. It can represent ill omen. It can represent Ishmael. But, biblically, it can also represent the inheritance of the priesthood. The thirteenth tribe, in a sense, were the Levites, who were God's portion. Recall that the tribe of Joseph was split into

Ephraim and Manasseh, making thirteen tribes. Twelve of the tribes had an inheritance in the promised land, but to the Levites, the Lord said, "...*the LORD is his inheritance*" (Duet. 10:9). So, in this case, thirteen represented a blessing of spiritual inheritance. The Levites were given thirteen cities as an inheritance. One more example is Matthias, the thirteenth apostle, selected to replace Judas who went his own way. Matthias brought order to the disruption brought about through Judas' rebellion.

Chapter 7

The Nature of Prophecy

W HAT IS THE NATURE of prophecy in prophetic ministry? When a word is given, people may be in danger of misunderstanding the word if they do not understand God's prophetic nature. If we do not understand prophecy in light of the nature of God, we risk misjudging a true word from God as false. The spirit of prophecy is the testimony of Jesus (Rev. 19:10).

A pastor or a teacher will generally minister to the needs of people from the perspective of their given offices. A prophet, however, must have a different measuring line. A prophet must make judgments from the perspective of the person's present circumstances and make the connection to a divine perspective which has been revealed. God approaches us where we are presently, but unless we receive a prophetic vision of where we need to be, we wander aimlessly. The Bible says that without vision, the people wander aimlessly (Prov. 29:18).

The prophetic word forewarns us of the future so that we can be prepared for that day. A prophetic word bolsters the waning soul to put it back on firm ground. It strengthens. It keeps us strong because that word lets us see. It gives a picture in the mind's eye and lets us see that which is now invisible.

The main reason the Lord allows the Church to have the prophetic word is so that we may adjust and prepare.

Comfort, yes, comfort My people! says your God. Speak comfort to Jerusalem, and cry out to her, that her warfare is ended, that her iniquity is pardoned; for she has received from the Lord's hand double for all her sins. The voice of one crying in the wilderness: Prepare the way of the Lord; make straight in the desert a highway for our God. Every valley shall be exalted and every mountain and hill brought low; the crooked places shall be made straight and the rough places smooth; the glory of the Lord shall be revealed, and all flesh shall see it together; for the mouth of the Lord has spoken (Isa. 40:1-5).

At the time Isaiah prophesied this word, it was all foretelling of future events. Presently, some of this prophecy has come to pass and some is still future. The first portion of this passage speaks of the list of sins and iniquities which are to be folded over and covered. They will not be seen anymore. The prophetic word says they are paid for; they are doubled over and out of sight. This word was given even though, at that time, the fulfillment was still future. We must be able to discern what is completed and what is still future for both prophecies in Scripture, as well as the prophetic word today. In Matthew 3:3, Jesus said that John the Baptist was the voice of one crying in the wilderness of whom Isaiah had prophesied. Isaiah's written prophecies prepared the way for John, and the spoken words of John, in turn, prepared the way for the Lord.

....

Chapter 8

Spiritual "Con Men"

A PROPHET WILL ALWAYS be somewhat suspected and scrutinized because it is necessary with prophecy to discern and judge the word and its application. I like to say that all those appointed to the prophetic office are commissioned to be "con men." In the natural, we call someone a "con" if he attempts to convince people that something that is not true, is true. However, in a positive way and in a spiritual sense, a prophetic person is often called upon to speak of things that are not, as though they are. The first person needing convincing is the prophetic person himself. The prophet must convince himself to speak boldly with faith what was received, even if full understanding is not available.

This describes a spiritual "con man."

There are nine "cons" of prophetic ministry:

1. To convince
2. To confess
3. To consult
4. To confer
5. To consecrate
6. To confirm
7. To confront
8. To contend
9. To convict

1. To convince. As stated previously, the first person needing convincing will be the person called to deliver a word. But, faith comes by hearing the word. Abraham was the main one to be convinced of the prophetic word brought to him. "...*And being fully convinced that what He had promised He was also able to perform*" (Rom. 4:21).

2. To confess before men and angels, to proclaim, to speak forth, to call out, to herald, to announce, to foretell. Nehemiah 6:7 says,

> *And you have also appointed prophets to proclaim concerning you at Jerusalem, saying, "There is a king in Judah!" Now these matters will be reported to the king. So come, therefore, and let us consult together.*

The prophets proclaimed and confessed before men, but then they also consulted together.

3. To consult. Prophetic people need to consult with the Lord. Remember that Elijah said, "The God before whom I stand..." and Elisha said, "The God before whom I stand...." They were able to consult with the Lord and, therefore, counsel those in authority who came to consult with them. The reason that David would consult with Nathan or consult with Samuel was because they, as prophets, were on God's "board." They went and listened to the counsel of the Lord and would bring that counsel before men. So, they consulted with God, and they consulted with those in authority.

4. To confer. A prophet will confer, which is to bestow, grant, award, or confer upon. An example is Elijah conferring upon Elisha the mantle that he had. He was passing it on and entrusting Elisha with it. First Kings 19:15-16 says,

> *Then the Lord said to him: "Go, return on your way to the wilderness of Damascus; and when you arrive, anoint Hazael as king over Syria. Also you shall anoint Jehu the son of Nimshi as king over Israel. And Elisha the son of Shaphat of Abel Meholah you shall anoint as prophet in your place."*

5. To consecrate means to set apart, to sanctify, to bless. Leviticus 8:12 says, "*And he poured some of the anointing oil on Aaron's head and anointed him, to consecrate him.*" In Exodus 40:13, it says that until Aaron was consecrated, he could not stand in the office of the prophet. We need the prophetic office to consecrate saints to the gifts which they are called to walk in. This is seen throughout the Word of

God. It is the prophetic ministry that calls out the gifts. Even if a person has the gift already, is working in it, and God is working in it, that person still should be consecrated into that call, allowing him to walk in it with empowerment and prophetic release.

6. To confirm means to sanctify or affirm, to authenticate. Acts 15:32 says, *"And Judas and Silas, being prophets also themselves, exhorted the brethren with many words and confirmed them."* The word *confirmed* is the Greek word *episterizo*. This word is always used in connection with the prophetic ministry in the New Testament. *Sterizo* is the word *establish*. This word is used in light of the apostolic ministry. Apostles establish; prophets confirm. This is the proper order within the foundation of the Church (Eph. 2:20). Without the prophetic word, there is no confirmation. Every true prophetic word will either confirm or be confirmed.

7. To contend means to have a contest, to charge, to clash, to do battle. First Timothy 1:18 says,

> *This charge I commit to you, son Timothy, according to the prophecies previously made concerning you, that by them you may wage the good warfare.*

Paul gave a charge to Timothy through a prophetic word which helped him to contend and do warfare.

8. To confront is to challenge, battle, or encounter. In First Kings 18, Elijah came before the people after the prophets of Baal had spent all day trying to call down fire from heaven, and he said, *"How long will you falter between two opinions? If the Lord is God follow Him. But if Baal then follow him."* But, they answered not a word. Elijah was confronting them. He was challenging them. Conviction follows confrontation.

9. To convict connotes a convincing or persuading. First Corinthians 14:24 says, *"But if all prophesy, and an unbeliever or an uninformed person comes in, he is convinced by all, he is convicted by all."* When an unbeliever or an uninformed person comes in and the people prophesy over that person, that person is convinced and convicted.

Chapter 9

How to Begin to Prophesy

WHILE THIS MATERIAL was written with a view toward those who have walked in the prophetic and have a desire to grow in this grace, it will likely also be read by others with an interest in the prophetic, but little or no experience. Since the Scriptures are clear that we all may prophesy, it seems appropriate to at least touch on the subject of how to begin to prophesy in a practical sense. However, let me say that an entire study could be completed on this subject alone.

To begin, let me suggest that the place to practice prophecy is not before the entire congregation on Sunday morning or at other large gatherings. This would not make any more sense than attempting to learn proficiency in football by trying to play your first game at the Super Bowl. I would like to suggest intercession, either in one's prayer closet or intercessory meetings, as a natural place to begin to stir up the prophetic gifting. Understand that prophecy does not come by the will of man, but by the will of God. Nevertheless, we may place ourselves in a position where His will intersects with our actions. By stirring up our spirit in intercession, the spirit of prophecy will usually be released. Often, in intercession, our spiritual senses will become more attuned to the prophetic Spirit of God.

For some, visions may begin as "thought visions." Often, impressions will come into our spirits or into our minds from the spirit. I suggest that you speak these things out loud or verbalize through prayer what is inspired in your heart by what you see. If you sense something in your body at a time like this, do not automatically assume that it is physical, because the Spirit will often communicate discernment of spiritual matters in this fashion. If you suddenly feel oppression or depression, it may be discernment for someone in the room, someone you have been praying for or perhaps your community. Try identifying these feelings, and then pray accordingly. If the feeling lifts, it is usually the Spirit's way of saying, "That's it. That's what I wanted you to pray." If you are sensing the Spirit of God desiring to speak through you, speak out the words. You will not generally receive the entire word before it is spoken, but rather one or two words or an impression to speak. As you speak, the Spirit will communicate the message through you, often as a prophetically inspired prayer.

Once a person becomes comfortable praying prophetically, it is a simple change to bring forth a message from

God for edification, exhortation, or comfort. Often, we are hesitant to speak without analyzing each word carefully first. But, in the context in which we are speaking—beginning to prophesy—this can be counterproductive. We are often hesitant to speak something which we do not understand for fear of being wrong, looking foolish, or perhaps praying something which we fear might not be God's will. However, prophecy usually cannot be understood until after it is spoken. I have learned a powerful example from the life of our Lord Jesus which I offer as a suggestion to assist in speaking and remove the need to evaluate each word. Jesus ended His praying in the garden by saying, *"...nevertheless not My will, but Yours, be done"* (Luke 22:42). I call this "God's line item veto," and praying this releases us to speak freely, knowing that we have asked God to disregard any words which were ours and not His. I have found that this knowledge brings a peace from which the Spirit of God can speak forth without hindrance from our insecurities.

CONCLUSION

For everything that God does, there is an antithesis in the enemy's camp. What God would do with love, the devil would do with lust. The opposite of the spirit of prophecy is a spirit of control. We are not to quench the Spirit, yet things should be done decently and in order. The antithesis of decently and in order is control. Paul said in Second Corinthians 12:9 that his strength was made perfect in weakness. His human strength was made perfect in realizing how weak he was in the flesh and then relying upon the Lord. He said, "For when I am weak then I am strong." These paradoxes are confusing to the natural mind because the natural man cannot receive the things of the Spirit (1 Cor. 2:14). Neither can the carnal Christian receive them because his mind is after the things of the world (Rom. 8:5,6). So, the Spirit speaking to us can take our strength and perfect it in an attitude of weakness before Him. For when I am weak in myself, then I am strong in the Lord. So, my strength comes from weakness. As we humble ourselves in the sight of the Lord, He will raise us up. This is the place of strength (Phil. 2:13).

Control has its root in envy and covetousness, which is birthed from insecurity and lack of trust. What is lack of trust? It is not fearing God. It is not trusting in the Lord. To give place to a spirit of control shows that we are not living a life that is laid upon Him, like John who laid his head upon Jesus' breast. Even in our own lives, we must relinquish control to the Lord because He knows best.

In the Kingdom of God, he who wants to be first must be willing to be last. He who wants to be greatest must be least. He who is greatest has the most authority in a particular sense. The way to receive the most authority is to become the greatest servant. Proverbs 16:19 says, *"Better to be of a humble spirit with the lowly, than to divide the spoil with the proud."* With authority comes the potential for pride—the more authority, the more potential for pride. The same is true for success: the more success, the more potential for pride. Pride always goes before destruction (Prov. 16:18). Pride brings confusion to others. It will not release the power of God in His Kingdom, and it will take away your reward even though you may minister good gifts. Pride keeps us from receiving the rewards. You become a sounding brass and a tinkling cymbal because love is not the motive. Humility is a key. The Church is confused on the issue of the gift of prophecy, which is intended to edify, exhort, and comfort. The gift ministry of the prophet is to speak the word of God as a testimony of Jesus. If John only had edifying and comforting words spoken to him, he never would have written the book of Revelation. A number of the seven churches addressed in the opening chapters of this book received some fairly harsh rebukes which reflect this.

Romans 12:20 says,

Therefore if your enemy is hungry, feed him; if he is thirsty, give him a drink; for in doing so you will heap coals of fire on his head.

Sometimes, we naturally tend to have a vengeful spirit toward our enemies. We would like to see this poor guy getting *burned up* with our kindness. *Just kill him* with kindness. That is not what this passage is about. It must be understood that the Bible is an Eastern book. In the villages, there was a central fireplace as well as individual hearths either in the home or right outside the door of the home. In the morning, someone from each household would fetch some coals from the central fire and bring them back to the house to start their fire. There were no matches back then. They would use a pot to lay the coals in. This pot was then placed on top of a protective cloth on top of the head to be carried. We have all seen pictures from the East of women carrying things on their heads. The carrying of those hot coals in that pot actually warmed the whole body of the individual from the top on down. It was considered a desirable job. Thus, the image described here was intended to convey the idea of doing good to your enemy. What Paul is saying, then, is if we will be kind even to those who are our enemies, our kindness will warm their insides up. To heap coals of fire is a blessing, not a curse. We are not to burn our enemies up, but to keep giving them the blessings, to give them peace.

Jesus said to "bless those who curse you and pray for those who spitefully use you" (Luke 6:28). Although we may have been hurt in the past by people who did not understand the word of the Lord that came through us, we must heap upon them coals of love to warm their hearts. Perhaps you were beaten down. Perhaps you were even spoken against or called a false prophet. Perhaps the word was given perfectly. Perhaps you are in leadership, and someone has come to you and tried to tell you that you had better listen because "I have got the word of the Lord." You have the responsibility of the oversight of the people, and you have got the care of the church. You are looking out for the people, and you do not want them to receive something that they would have to deal with if it is not correct. So, you have got to be kind to those with a word and realize you have to raise these people up so we can have all five aspects of Christ's ministry gifts in operation.

We can have a true spirit of humility, of submission in ourselves and toward one another, by living for one another, by loving one another, and by allowing ourselves to die to ourselves so that we can live for Jesus Christ. The Master needs to be the Head of the Church once again. We need once again to hear His testimony out of His people. Out of the mouths of babes will come perfect praise.

The spirit of prophecy must be used with all the fruit of the spirit involved. We must always walk in love, whether we are received or whether we are rejected. It is more important to obey and walk in love than to obey alone. Out of that love will come faith. Out of that love will come prophecy. Out of that love will come the grace which He will build His tabernacle upon. Out of that love will come the prophetic mortar that will hold together the living stones. Out of that love will come the plumb line that we can use to build and draw the line in judgment and line up the plumb in righteousness (Isa. 28:17).

....

Chapter 10

Growing in the Prophetic Study Guide

Introduction

1. Spiritual ignorance (1 Cor. 12:1, 14:38, 2:10; Hos. 4:6; Prov. 11:9).

2. Difference between a prophet and a prophetic person:

   a. **Prophet** (Eph. 4:11,12). The Body of Christ has not yet been perfected, therefore, the five fold ministries must be functioning to carry this out. The prophet is a gift to the Body of Christ (v. 8). A prophet is specifically ordained by God to operate in that office (2 Cor. 10:18; Acts 13:2). A prophet speaks by inspiration regularly.

b. **Prophetic person**. There is no office with this description. The prophetic word given is a gift to the Body of Christ. There is no ordination by God to operate in this capacity, however, there is grace and encouragement to prophecy (1 Cor. 14:5,13,39). A prophetic person does not usually speak by inspiration on a regular basis, though he or she may be a prophet in training.

Chapter 1

1. A prophetic word can never contradict Scripture. The Bible is a more sure source of God's revelation than prophecy (2 Pet. 1:19). God allows Satan to have access to our minds if we position ourselves to refuse God's correction (2 Chron. 18:21,22). Satan is a spirit; he has a spiritual voice (1 Cor. 14:10). A Christian can be taken captive by Satan's voice (2 Tim. 2:25,26).

2. A prophetic word should be judged not only by Scripture, but also by other prophets (1 Cor. 14:29). The pure Word is tried by fire seven times (Ps. 12:6).

3. We need the prophetic voice in our midst (Acts 9:11; 1 Tim. 1:18; 2 Chron. 20:20; Amos 3:7). It is not an option (Eph. 4:11,12; 1 Cor. 14:5,13,39; 1 Thess. 5:19,20).

4. All believers may prophecy (1 Cor. 14:5,13,31,39), whereas, not all believers are prophets (1 Cor. 12:29).

Chapter 2

1. The gifts of the Spirit are given by God as He chooses, but we can position ourselves, by desire and

humility, to inspire God to give us these gifts (Jas. 4:6; 1 Cor. 12:11).

2. The character and abilities of the prophetic person must be mentored. Without the mature leading the immature, harsh words can do much damage to a church body. The soul of the prophet must be as pure as possible. Church leadership must take the responsibility of not only encouraging the prophetic, but also of honing away the chaff of resentment, anger, and frustration that often accompanies the prophetic.

Chapter 3

1. The prophet or prophetic person has as much responsibility to heed the word from God as any other believer. He or she has the same spiritual equipment as any other believer to implement the word in his or her life.

2. The RARA principle is often short circuited. Once receiving a revelation, a novice prophetic person will usually assume an authority that has not been given or earned by leadership. This principle revolves around proper relationship. God has set up authority structures in society, in the Church, and even in heaven. Unless authority is honored, God will not honor a servant's desire to be used by Him. If the RARA principle is adhered to and the church leadership refuses to hear the Word of the Lord, the proper response is to intercede. Writing down the word and submitting it to leadership is also an accepted alternative. Be careful of manipulation. A true word from the Lord can be distorted by an improper motive.

Chapter 4

1. Once a word is received from the Lord, it is the responsibility of the prophet or prophetic person to ask the Lord what to do with it. Should you keep it to yourself and pray it back to God? Give it to the congregation? Give it only to a certain person or a select few? Write it down only? Ask the Lord what to do. The delivery should be only what the Lord says. Do not add your own commentary. Manipulative "hooks" should be avoided, such as "the Lord told me to tell you..." or "thus says the Lord" (when the Lord didn't say it). Once the message is delivered, shut up and sit down. It is the purview of leadership to do anything with it. Don't be upset if they don't act on it. If nobody else acts on it and you know it is the Lord speaking, then YOU act on it.

2. As believers, we have been given individual gifts (1 Cor. 7:7). This does not imply we cannot acquire more than what we are originally given. The parable of the unprofitable servant tells us we should do more than what is expected of us (Luke 17:7-10). If you are a *nabiy* prophetic person, ask the Lord if you can be a *chozeh* type. If you desire it and God allows you to, then set yourself in a position to receive the grace to carry it out. The same thing is true for the *roeh* category.

Chapter 5

1. Revelations received by open vision or by simple impression, and everything in between, are all of God. They should be treated as such. God can speak

to a seasoned prophet by a simple impression if He so chooses. We should not place any prophet or prophetic person on a pedestal because they received a "higher" form of revelation than what is common.

2. Spiritual pride is inappropriate on any level. Remember, Scripture is a more sure word of prophecy, and we all have the Word.

Chapter 6

1. The interpretation of a revelation can be instantaneous or it may progressively unfold itself over time. It may involve others. If you don't get the interpretation right away, it may be appropriate to give it to other prophetic people for their input. We see in part, but together, often, we get the whole picture.

2. The Lord sometimes chooses to use symbols, pictures, even riddles to communicate to us. Why doesn't He speak in a straight forward manner (Matt. 13:10)? Sometimes, someone will receive a picture, but not a direct word. Sometimes, the process of finding out the interpretation of a revelation bears more fruit than the revelation itself. E.W. Bullinger's book *Numbers in Scripture* is a good source of information regarding numbers and symbolic meaning.

Chapter 7

1. Unfortunately, today, there are not many venues for a prophet in training or a prophetic person to "practice." Often the Church expects him or her to get it right without providing training. Therefore, the

prophetic person must spend much time in prayer and intercession to build up that practice time.

2. In light of the possibility of getting it wrong, when prophesying to another person, it is good to leave him with the biblical caveat, "In the mouth of two or three witnesses shall every word (*rhema*) be established" (2 Cor. 13:1). Tell the person that he should not act on the word unless he has received a confirming word from other sources.

Chapter 8

1. There will always be an element of doubt about any word within the heart of a prophetic person. This is normal.

2. We should constantly be checking our motives, our Scriptural understandings, and our hearts. When Peter walked on the water, his spirit was saying, "Go for it!" while his soul was saying, "You idiot! What are you doing?!"

Chapter 9

1. The person desiring to walk in the prophetic must be absolutely convinced that such a thing is available. If there is any doubt, there will not be the requisite faith to receive from God (Rom. 14:23). Therefore, it is important to answer any questions and quell any fears before proceeding. Testimonies may help in this process.

2. After a person is convinced that prophecy is possible, instruction should be given as to what to expect.

Initially, only a word or two are perceived in the spirit. As these are uttered, more are given until the entire message is complete. A good way to start is to ask God for an interpretation of a tongue (1 Cor. 14:13) to edify, comfort, and exhort (v. 3). If the person does not speak in tongues, this does not disqualify them from prophecy, however, it may be a good opportunity to lead them into this blessing (Luke 11:13). This can be done in a small group or privately. Practice dispels fears and creates confidence. A supportive atmosphere is essential. Everyone must feel they will not be judged and condemned if they make a mistake.

3. Although prophecy, in a simple sense, is to exhort, comfort, and edify (1 Cor. 14:3), a prophetic word can also take on an edge of admonition. An example of this is the book of Revelation. This happens more in the case of a mature prophet. Few five fold ministers are only one of the five. They are often combinations of them. For instance, a prophet might also be very didactic (a teacher). A prophetic intercessor may have a little bit of prophet in him; thus, sometimes, his words may take on the hue of admonition. This is normal.

About the Author

....

L LOYD PHILLIPS PRESENTLY resides in Missoula, Montana with his wife and two children. He is the senior minister of Fellow Laborers' International Church and the apostle and director of the Fellow Laborers' International Network (FLInt Net)—a growing network of churches, ministries, and intercessors in the United States and other nations. Lloyd has been teaching, preaching, and researching the Word and ways of God for more than twenty-five years. He travels and teaches seminars and ministers in order that both individuals and churches may be established. His ministry supplies covering and direction to associated churches and ministry works known as the FLAMES (Fellow

Laborers' Association of Ministries). He administers a growing tape ministry, including the NETS (Necessary Equipping in Truth Series) training program. This audio teaching program assists the Christian in his or her journey from a believer into discipleship, on to stewardship in the Kingdom, and finally into the ministry of our Lord Jesus Christ.

Lloyd has a unique ability to discover overlooked and under-expanded truths and to enlighten and bring the Christian into a greater awareness of the presence of God and a greater understanding of one's personal call to serve the Lord. He is an active leader in his city's ministerial association, as well as a member of various ministry associations and apostolic networks. In all of this, he draws strength from helping to equip the people of God to walk in the power, love, and freedom which is given to them by our heavenly Father.

The Fellow Laborers' International Network
Lloyd C. Phillips, Director
P.O. Box 113
Missoula, MT 59806
Phone (406) 251-8580 FAX (406) 251-7035

E-mail: flintnet@flintnet.org
Web: http://www.flintnet.org